Walking the Property Line

Messages From
Nature's Sanctuary

Books by Steven O. Ludd

Confronting the Politics of Gridlock
Revisiting the Founding Visions in Search of Solutions

Reflections Off the Lake
Poems on Life, Love and Democracy

Walking the Property Line
Messages From Nature's Sanctuary

Walking the Property Line

Messages From
Nature's Sanctuary

Steven O. Ludd

Distinction Press
Waitsfield, Vermont

Walking the Property Line
Messages From Nature's Sanctuary

Steven O. Ludd

Distinction Press
Waitsfield, Vermont 05673
distinctionpress.com

Book design by RSBPress, Waitsfield, Vermont

Tradepaper ISBN 978-1-937667-34-4
Hardcover ISBN 978-1-937667-35-1

Library of Congress Control Number: 2023922124

For tomorrow's children

Acknowledgments

I have been blessed with support for this book by Kitty Werner of Distinction Press. She has guided me through the imperatives of manuscript production and has offered her creative talents for the design of the book's cover.

My wife, Oksana M. Ludd has also provided unyielding support for the project. Her commitment to the values expressed throughout the book provided the energy required for its completion.

The illustrations within the book are the creations of Dan Blaushild. Dan is a multi-talented graphic artist who presently is a member of the Film Unit for *Saturday Night Live*. That he was willing to participate in this project is deeply appreciated.

Ian Sheldon Ludd, my son, and my daughter-in-law, Krista Lynn Johnson Ludd, have also provided the necessary motivation to start and complete this journey. Indeed, this book is dedicated to them and others of their generation who also are committed to the protection of our environment and of democracy across the world.

Contents

Introduction

Like droplets of dew shimmering across the meadows in early morning sunlight, poetry and prose can also nourish our souls with love and compassion as we make our way throughout each day.

It encourages us to stop, dig deep, and listen to the magical rhythms pulsating from Mother Earth — as we join together to protect her wondrous treasures.

Messages from

Nature's Sanctuary

Walking the Property Line

I ventured out one day in an effort to survey
The property I called mine. Filled with pride
That my life could be measured somehow by
The number of Maples, Birches, and Pines.
But as I continued my journey, I began to
Recognize the shallowness of such thoughts.

The truth is I am simply this cycle's inhabitant
Of this parcel of Earth's crust — A mere caretaker
Of Mother Earth's prodigies. An Executor, if you will,
Of her everlasting Trust — Allowed to breathe in the sweet
Smell of the Pine. And to possess the sublime feelings attached
To this strip of land bequeathed to me by those who came before
Flocking here from distant shores seeking liberty —
fleeing from Tyranny.

Sadly, too often we did not understand that this land needed
To be shared not taken. That there was much to be learned from
Those who also came upon this land in their migration.
Who too confronted the age-old dilemma of living in peace with
Others who also challenged their right to reap the treasures which
Mother Earth had placed before them.

Indeed, the further I walked the property line, the more I began
To understand that my original claim of ownership had to be tempered
By my membership in the club of humanity. But one of many Earth's
Citizens trying to fulfill our individual missions. It only re-enforced
My commitment to protect Earth's spectacular beauty — It was my
Duty for those who come after.

What a privilege, I thought, it is to walk the property line.

On Morning Walks

They come every morning for the nourishment of their souls.
Searching for silent messages emanating from the little pond.
They listen to the sounds of tadpoles scurrying in the water.
Hoping that, like the pond fed by the surrounding springs, they
Too would be constantly refreshed by the majesty of Nature.

They come seeking guidance from the silent messages sent
By the surrounding trees — praying that the Oracle of the forest
Will show them the path to eternity.

They listen to the sounds of the Wind ruffling the leaves of
The forest's canopy. They feel the soft raindrops dancing
Across their faces and creating ripples on the pond.

For an instant they feel the timeless beauty of now and
Begin to understand the gift they have been given.

Their only wish is that others would also listen.

An Early Morning Performance

I awoke this morning to the honking of geese in flight
Circling around a nearby pond. They signaled to all who pass by
That they would soon be gliding down into their seasonal home
Where they had already prepared a nest for their tiny prodigies.

Needless to say, I could not remain in bed. I needed to observe
what
I knew would be a wondrous spectacle. No ticket required.
Another
Of Nature's freebies.

Concerned that my presence might disturb their predetermined
Plans
to forage and protect their fluffy ducklings now prancing in
the water, I remained at a distance — just far enough away to
Observe the magical performance and the grace of Mother Nature's
Creatures on this beautiful emerging day.

But I could not help but silently
Applaud these wondrous guardians of this year's new arrivals and
hope that
My observation would not interfere with their decision to remain
and return
Once again next year.

Secret Sounds

Deep within the forest
There flows over a granite ledge
A little waterfall.

It is not much more than a Spring
Overflow of Winter's ice and snow.

It certainly cannot compete with
Niagara or Victoria in their powerful
Bursts of liquid spray.

But to those few who wander
On early Spring mornings, it brings
A rhythmic sound as it slowly searches
For more passages to the woodland floor.

Can a humble wanderer ask for more?

A Magic Wand

If I had a magic wand, I would slow down the sand
In the hour glass.
I would cast an invisible net to capture all the dreams
Filled with images of love's longing to be placed in my memory
Not to be lost before morning.

I would sprinkle droplets of white crystals
Containing memories of love on all my brothers and sisters —
Red, Yellow, Brown, Black, and White — To help them not lose sight
Of promises not yet kept. Of our collective obligation to protect Earth's
wonders
For those who come after.

I would remind them of the smell of the Ocean's salty air.
Of the majesty of geese in orderly formation heading to
Their southernly destinations. Of the wonders of Earth's waterfalls
Spraying their mist so essential for the forest canopy.
And, for the biodiversity amongst all creatures great and small
living below —
Acting out the balance so essential for life's survival.

I would send messages to all who would listen
Of the miraculous rhythms so long ago given.

An Unplanned Trek

It was a quiet morning. The Sun had just begun to rise.
But something seemed to be telling me that it would be wise
To enter the forest and answer some silent call.

So, through the Forest's underbrush I trod —
Trying not to damage the newly emerging Fiddlehead ferns
Or trample on some unsuspecting frog.

After what seemed to be a haphazard march through
The saplings of Maple and Pine, I spotted signs of a small
But freshly made path.

Having ventured this far without rhyme or reason for the
Unplanned trek, I decided to follow the slightly trampled
Ground of the woodland floor.

Who knows, I thought, maybe it will lead me to some secret
Cave inhabited by a lonely creature trying, like me, to find
Sanctuary from men filled with hate.

But then I reconsidered. More likely the trail was shaped
By one who has a route in mind. To plot a course to see what
Might exist beyond the Forest's protective curtain and overhanging
Canopy.

Its path was most certainly an attempt to breach the safety
Provided by the undergrowth and surrounding trees — catapulting
Its creator into the mysteries that new vistas may provide.

Suddenly, the trail was at its end. A little meadow stood before
Me. It was filled with sunflowers and yarrow. It was then that I
Felt a kinship with the little creature who carved the way
Through the forest that day.

While I may never come again, the unspoken advice it
Provided to me will forever stay.

A Late Winter Surprise

The cascading snow engulfs the woodlot
And old house with soft white flakes
Gently falling as if they were in a snow
Globe just being shaken.

The landscape miraculously transitions
From the brown muddy terrain that late
Winter thaws provide to a refreshing new
Blanket of white.

It is a brief reminder that Spring has yet
To arrive. And, to be patient. Just enjoy
The magical ride that Mother Nature provides.

On a Blistering Winter Morning

It was a bitter cold and gloomy morning
When most chose to remain in bed, that
A hearty group of men walked through freshly
Fallen snow to the little country store located
Below on the mountain's floor.

They came this morning as they do almost
Every day. To taste the freshly brewed coffee and
Homemade pastries and sit around an old potbelly stove
Which sometimes spits out steam making it difficult to see.

They banter back and forth their thoughts of the emerging
Day. Some are shopkeepers from the village a few miles away.
Others are workmen and farmers clad in their daily attire. Ready
For their tasks of the day.

Sprinkled amongst those on their way to work are a few retired
Old-timers eager to listen to their younger neighbors and occasionally
Interject their observations on the subjects of conversation each
morning.

Every once in a while, politics finds its way into the discussions.
Sometimes raising the commentary to a level of heat
Competing with that emitted from the stove.

But it is almost always the case that one particular senior
Citizen, after listening to the increasingly heated dialogue, is
Depended upon to lower the temperature with a story
And an old adage sprinkled with a joke or two.

Those in attendance always know he will bring the
Morning debates to a level of humor and friendly banter —
Much to the relief of the store's owner who, while often
Offering his opinions, wanted most of all to sell more percolating
Coffee and pastries bulging from bins lining the walls of the old store.

This morning's discussion which raised to the level of intense debate,
Concerned a group of citizens who were unwilling to listen to
Other community members regarding the potential of proposed
New home development within what some believed to be portions
Of the surrounding mountains negatively impacting their pristine beauty.

Eventually, the group turned to the old man for his opinion. Knowing the
Personalities involved in the debate, he began by agreeing with portions
Of the two competing arguments. Then the resident sage smiled
And responded that compromise needed to be found and offered a way.

He said jobs needed to be encouraged to support the local economy
And would be found with the construction of new homes.
But he said it must be agreed that any development must be carefully
Planned and monitored by the community in order to preserve the scenic
Beauty which attracts individuals from across the country to their mountain
Paradise.

He then reminded all in attendance that they needed to be careful not
To "destroy the goose that laid the golden eggs."
He then encouraged them
To dismiss the commentary of some within the community
Unwilling to compromise by reminding those sitting around the
Potbelly stove that, "You can bring a horse to water, but you
Can't make it drink."

Almost all seemed to concur. And, at least for now, were
Satisfied with the old man's advice. And, from the smiles on
Their faces, it appeared that the coffee and conversations
Were well worth the effort of rising to confront the cold
And ice and the tasks of the day.

The resident sage too was silently pleased that he
Was allowed to be part of the early morning morality play
On this bitter winter's day.

An Unmatched Performance

The daffodils and tulips have arrived. They are sending
Messages that they will stay for a while and frolic in the
Early Spring sunlight — as we await the next act of Mother
Nature's four-part play.

Oh, how wonderful it is to greet each day with the
Emergence of perennials hidden deep within her
Breast. All waiting to appear upon the stage — providing
Unmatched performances for their allotted time — before
They must rest.

The colors of variegated hostas — green and white — shimmering
In the early morning sunlight. Purple shoots of peonies just rising
From their Winter's rest. Lilies of the Valley scrambling across the
The garden floor sending sweet fragrances to all who venture by.
Reminding them that there is much more to come in this first act
Of the Seasons.

What a joy it is to have secured tickets to the front row
Of this performance. And to be able to reap the bounty
Of what once was ice and snow.

Under House Arrest

Invaded by the existential
While dusting the dining-room table.

Spring Cleaning

I went to the garden today to remind
The emerging weeds that they cannot stay.

It is that time in the cycle where we understand
That a cleansing must take place. A time when we,
Like the landscape, must begin a refresh.

To begin to discard the fears that a long cold winter has brought.
And to start the planting of new seeds — to bolster our
Thoughts of beautiful arrivals which Mother Nature will
Provide — If only we will assist in guaranteeing that all her
Treasures will survive.

Grateful

One early morning I looked through the window
To see what the day had in store for me.

Like a child on Christmas morning, I could not restrain
The excitement I felt as I gazed at the new sprouting
Buds of the surrounding shrubs.

Like presents wrapped under the Christmas tree, each new
Arrival called out to me to choose it first for my attention and
Appreciation. But, like parents who are asked, who amongst all
Of their Children they love the most, I too understood that I possessed
Enough love to shower them all with my unrelenting attention
And everlasting admiration of their special roles in
Mother Nature's Master plan.

The Migration Begins

They are back again pecking at the still frozen
Ground. Searching for tiny morsels, turning
Their heads round and round to the turf.
Listening for a sound that would confirm
that their next meal will be found.

They have every right to flock to the woodland
Floor now exploding with insects galore.
These yearly migrants have also survived the
The Winter's ice and snow. So, they have returned
To reclaim their integral role in Nature's reoccurring
Theme.

But this marauding band of robins is not interested
In the existential. Their only thoughts concern those
Eager to await their return — with the rewards of
Foraging on this wonderful Spring morning.

Dedication

Across the clearing at the far end of the meadow
A black and white creature moved with careful
Deliberation.

She studied the reaction that her movements made
By the flock of sheep she has been tasked to collect and protect
Again today.

Her actions are often directed by a call or a whistle
From her master. But this time is different. The farmer
Has not yet reached the pasture. And she has spotted
Danger.

Hidden — crouching low in the grass behind the flock —
Is a coyote.

She instinctively understands that she must quickly
Surround the sheep and herd them from the pasture
To the safety of the fenced farm.

Generations of careful breeding now provides the most
Amazing performance one can observe. Flashes of black and
White images running from left and right encircle the flock
Creating a formation which responds to her every movement
Guiding them to the safety of the fenced barn yard.

She has displayed an independent decisiveness rarely spotted
Without human interaction. The loyal Border Collie has saved
The day. And is welcomed by her grateful master with
deep affection.

More Performances to Come

It is late in the symphony's performance
And some wish for the curtain to be drawn
To provide the last applause for a magical time
Filled with the angelic sounds of Chopin and the
Absorbing melodies of Rachmaninoff.

They have accepted their fate — that where there
Is a beginning there is always an end.

While they are correct that all things of this time and space
Must eventually conclude, so is it true that the end of each
Performance brings wonderful expectations of new creations —
Endlessly provided by those who translate the pulsating sounds
Emitted throughout the Universe into musical scores — for
Future generations to hear. And to behold the beauty which
Surrounds all who are willing to stop and listen.

Sadly, what some in the audience are unable or unwilling
To understand is that they too can be interpreters of the
Cosmic melodies and can create their own musical scores.
If only they would open the door to the beautiful rhythms
Awaiting them when the next curtain is raised and new
Concerts are performed.

One Step at A Time

I was tapped on the shoulder yesterday
By some invisible force reminding me that
It was time to venture outside to play
Amongst the sweet smell of the blossoming
Lilac and the bearded iris standing tall in
The morning's sunlight.

As I approached the newly planted dogwoods
And forsythia, I was overcome by the spectacular
Beauty it was my privilege to nurture and protect.
Humbled by the task before me, I wondered what
One man could do to guarantee for the children who
Come after, the gifts that surround us all?

But then I remembered that each journey starts one
Step at a time. I then determined that this morning
Would be the beginning of my obligation to tend this
Little garden entrusted to me.

I now understood that this day was just the beginning
Of my responsibility to be a part of Nature's plan for all
Mankind to protect and preserve her treasures for those who
Come after.

Nature's Sanctuary

It is where the bluebirds come to nest
Where my spirit always rests.
Where throughout the day hummingbirds
Come to taste the sweet nectar of the blossoming
Rose of Sharon.

It is the place where the gardens burst with color from
Spring to Autumn and brings the beauty of Winter snowfalls
Which wrap the landscape with a blanket of white linen
Magically transforming the woodland with crystals of ice
On cold winter days.

It is where the pine and birches provide a backdrop for
The beautiful blue sky above. Where they send their never-ending
Messages of love. Where they defiantly proclaim that Mother
Nature's power still overcomes whatever misdeeds man has done.

And that, regardless of our fears in the years to come, they will
Provide symbols for all who fight to protect them and those
Who seek freedom.

Sunrise

Many years have past
And the tasks of life's obligations
Have taken their toll.

The evolution of the soul's demands
Have slowly depleted the energy
Of youth.

Yet, each morning brings the wonderment
Of the rising Sun and the sounds of each
Emerging day.

The pulsating rhythms not heard
In my youth are now felt
Emanating from Mother Earth.

The sound of raindrops softly tapping
On the window pane and dancing across
The roof. The rustling of the old Maple's
Leaves announcing that a new day has almost begun
As it awaits the arrival of the Sun.

Oh, Helios, thank you for another day — reminding
Us all that whatever sadness tomorrow may bring
Will be overcome with thoughts of love both from
Days passed and from those we create today.

An Interested Observer

My assignment for the day is to watch
The Sparrows play. To be a referee of sorts
Between the chattering of aggressive squirrels
Pushing their way into a newly shaped hole
In the old Maple tree created by Red Capped
Woodpeckers in an effort to house their newly acquired
Stash of nuts.

The Black Capped chickadees, however, remain unperturbed
By the loud chatter. One after one they continue to claim
Squatters' rights — sending a message to all that this
Disagreement may end in a fight.

I think I will sit this one out. Mother Nature is whispering
That this one is bigger than me. And that I might as well
Enjoy the show — after all, I have nowhere to go.

Travelers

They walk the ancient streets.
They view the vistas from lands' end.
They absorb the wonders of the world.
All in search for themselves.

Like innocent children who gaze in wonderment
At the emergence of the first buds
From Spring daffodils, they are in awe
Of Nature's gifts appearing on
Faraway shores.

Yet, their experiences are ephemeral — they are
Flashes of images sent to remind them
After they have departed — that now
They carry a heavy responsibility to join others
Who wander — in the battle to protect the
Beauty that they have been privileged to
Explore.

And, to understand, upon their return to
Native soil, the task to become more than
Mere observers in the fight to preserve
Earth's treasures.

Fire-Flies

It was getting dark. The Sun had set
After a long warm summer's day. A time
When most had settled in for the night.

But the children were far from any
Bedtime ritual — their excitement
Could barely be contained.

They had been given permission
To once again prepare their glass jars
With holes in their metal tops
For the mission ahead.

To rush out the door to the meadow
And to capture the fireflies just emerging
In the night's sky and to gently place them
In their jars.

They were told that like shooting stars, the
Fireflies that they collected were little messengers
Of love from a greater source. And, that they would
Light the Way for tomorrow's promises bringing more
Wonderous days of play.

Many summers have passed and the search for
Fireflies continues. What do you say? Have you
Found them? Or, do they no longer come to stay?

Patience

Hidden high on the mountain's crest
Lay the remains of snow and ice
Packed tight around a granite rock
Protruding through the surrounding
Flora and fauna just beginning to
Emerge from Winter's last surge.

Oh, how I want to encourage the
Undergrowth with its verdant
Carpet of early Spring flowers
By scrapping the remaining frozen
Soil — to set them all free. To rejoice
In the Sun and gentle warm wind breeze.

But I fear that my interference with
The cycles so magically created, will
Somehow disrupt a scheme designed
Millennia ago.

So, just like my soul, the mountain's flora and
Fauna will need to be patient as we await
Our predetermined destinies.

Digging

The task today is to dig six holes
In the Burning Bush bed — careful not
To go too deep.
Just far enough beneath
The soil's surface so that the root ball
Fits snuggly into the fertile bed and that
The roots of the newly acquired chrysanthemums
Can continue to spread and provide more of
their beautiful palette of colors.

Shimmering flashes of yellow and gold
Sometimes mixed with burgundy and purple
These late summer visitors bring a
Welcomed reminder that the hot and humid
Days of summer will soon give way to the magical
Cycle called Fall.

They send a message that our lives are inextricably
Entwined with the never-ending rhythms of Mother
Earth.

I think I will stop digging for a moment
And enjoy the wondrous display of the mums
On this gift of a day.

A Reminder

There is a place where dreams become reality.
Where love overcomes hate.
Where empathy abounds.
Where diversity in all things is crowned.

It is there where peace will be found
Amongst the new blossoming leaves
Which are rapidly responding to the
Sounds of creatures deep within the
Overhanging forest canopy.

It beckons us to listen and see
That we are a part of a magical symphony
In which we play — chord after chord —
The notes of the musical score assigned
To us.

A composition begun long ago immersed
In gentle rhythms. Directing us to the paths
Which we must follow along our journey
Through to the Milky Way.

For Tomorrow's Children

For Tomorrow's Children

We must join together for tomorrow's
Children. To protect their coming.
To guarantee their mornings. To wrap
Our arms around their dreams.

To leave a legacy of love. To reject hate.
To prepare the way for their journeys.
To join in solidarity in our efforts to
Preserve this wonderful blue marble
And all its treasures.

To remain engaged and refuse to succumb
To the illiterate rage.

To present them upon their arrival
With the sweet nectars that Mother
Earth provides — to all who recognize
Their obligation to sow the seeds of
Love and appreciation.

And to celebrate our opportunity to
Be part of this collective journey this
time around the Sun.

In Search for Answers

Far away on distant shores
They stare into the red and orange
Glow of bombs exploding into the
Night sky — signs of the continuing
War.

They try not to be hardened by thoughts
Of revenge. Yet, they understand that
The missiles shot down were meant
For them, their family, and their friends.
And while they recognize that
The present conflict may end, they know that
Their lives will never be the same.

How does one explain to the children
That love will overcome hate. But, that
Evil still exists. And that it must be confronted
And destroyed if the promises of Spring are
Are to come again?

How do they tell the children that the flower bulbs
Planted in the Fall will return and that Democracy
Will be achieved after all?

Tonight, a warm hug must suffice, as the children
Are put to bed — with loving reassurances that
Everything will be alright. And to sleep tight.
Slava Ukraini.

Sunset on the Water

It was a beautiful day. Filled with
sun, sand, and surf. And with thoughts
of friends far away.

As the Sun slowly reached the Ocean's
Horizon, the aqua blue of the sea began
To engulf the mellow orange/yellow glow
Of the setting Sun.

Suddenly there appeared an image
Of a massive window — framed by reflections
Off the incoming waves.

The window appeared to have smaller panes
Within it. Each providing flashing scenes with
Beautiful script — all different in form — but
All leading to one massive door. Slowly moving
To the shore.

Each pane contained visions of the Seers
Who have come before. All of whom offered
The keys to open the door.

Looking farther into the window with its
Various panes, it became clear that they
All merged into one beautiful message
For all to see. That there is a wondrous
Path for all humanity to live in
Everlasting harmony.

The spiritual guidance of our ancestors
Who walked Mother Earth millennia ago
Provided the backdrop for each image
Beckoning those on the shore to look
Closely — providing notice that there
Was more to see.

One pane flashed images of Siddartha
And his reminder of peaceful self-reflection.

Another was filled with observations from
The Tao Te Ching bringing understanding
Of the unity of opposites in the functioning
Of the universe.

A third window pane slowly scrolled through
The life and time of the man from Nazareth —
Stopping for short intervals, highlighting
Powerful visions of love and explaining how
To overcome hate.

The guidance of the Torah
Also appeared — as well as — the Koran — both
Providing insights on how to conduct one's
Life.

As the sun set behind the horizon into
The vastness of the sea, these images reminded
Me that, regardless of the cultural differences
From which each pane was constructed, that they
All sent a powerful message. One which is
Unmistakable to those willing to open their
Heart and mind.

That this journey we call life is filled with
Numerous doors through which we can enter
To celebrate our opportunities to be Children of
Light in the never-ending battle for love to overcome
Hate.

Let us not wait.

The Assignment

"I am — all that was and that will ever be."
The voice said.

"I will be your messenger." She responded.

"Shower them with love." The voice continued.

"I will bring them the beauty of the universe."
She answered.

"Show them the way through the darkness of
Hate." The voice urged her.

"I will guide them through." She promised.

"Help them understand that they can be
Children of the stars — not simply what they
Think they are." The voice pleaded.

"I will make it my mission. I will help them
Heal." She reassured.

"Show them how to find me." The voice
Suggested.

"I will teach them to know their inner strength
And how to overcome hate through
Each season — to understand the cycles.
I will prepare the way."
Said Mother Earth — on the initial Day.

QUERY

I have found myself outside your door.
Wondering if there is more to know and
See.

You have provided me with the wonders
Of life. To have felt the misery of poverty
And the rewards of success.

I have experienced the warmth of love
And the despair which brings death.

But as I knock on your door, I ask, what
More must be done? Before I come to
Meet thee?

Have I fulfilled the promises made by those
Souls who have come before — who took up
The sword to guarantee that I would reap
The bounty of the seeds of liberty — sown
Before?

What more must be done to assist in the
Evolution of men's souls to reach the perfection
Which must be attained so that peace can become
Reality for all humanity?

A Time for Cleansing

Like the branches of white birches bent
To the ground after a heavy wet winter
Snowfall, our democracy has been also
Twisted and burdened by unscrupulous
Grifters for too long.

But it is also true that with the assistance
Of a caretaker who gently clears the snow
And ice from the birch's limbs, so too
Can we cleanse, through the use of the
Rule of law, all those who endanger the
Quest for a country dedicated to justice
For all.

Gotham

Oh, great city filled with buildings
Which touch the sky — billowing towers
Displaying architectural creativity
Standing as symbols of the power
Of commerce and of immigration.

You represent an unrelenting desire to
To inspire your inhabitants with the
Energy to challenge the unknown of
Each day with the confidence that
Whether success or failure is met,
The power of the city will carry them
Through to the next opportunity and
Next sunset.

You do so with an appreciation that
Humanity is served best by understanding
The pulsating beat that a multitude of
Cultures brings. And to rejoice in your
History of welcoming all who seek liberty.

Despite your trials and tribulations and
Your pretense of toughness, you have always
Wrapped your arms around those who are
Fleeing tyranny.

Oh, Gotham, never forget you have carried
The flame of hope and of what makes America
A bastion of light.

May we never lose sight of the fact
That at the core of this Nation, filled
With immigrants from across the world,
You are a symbol of our everlasting might.

A Little Garden

There appeared in the middle
Of urban plight a little garden —
Created, what it seemed, overnight.

It glowed amongst the darkness of
The surrounding tenements. Filled with
New immigrants from around the world.
All struggling to find their way.

Cramped together — challenged by language
Barriers and cultural differences — hoping to
Secure their families for a new day.

Amidst the fear and depression that constantly
Knocks on their door, their children's laughter
Reminds them that they must endure the back-
Breaking labor which they have secured for the
Family's survival.

The neighbors have little in common, yet, they
Have found one endeavor which resonates with
Them all. The planting of a garden.

It will not only produce gifts of Nature's bounty,
But it will also necessitate co-operation. And in
So doing, it will develop an appreciation of each
Others commitment to the loving care required
For its creation and protection.

Therefore, at the end of each day's
Physical exhaustion from their often
Menial work tasks, they return to the
Little plot of earth — in search of memories
Of home which often reminded them of
When they scraped the barren soil in an
Effort to provide sustenance but for one
More day.

Yet, they thought this little garden will
Be different. It will be bountiful. Because
It was born, not out of fear, but out of love
And respect. They believed that the combined
Efforts of their neighbors would provide all
With a secure future.

So, each night after work they took turns at
Ripping and replacing the harden city turf
With compost secured by collecting the discarded
Remains of each gardener's produce. They were
Confident that they had prepared the soil for seed.

While the city lights only provided partial illumination
On their small parcel of earth, each gardener knew
Every section of turf. Each night they took turns, with
Flashlights in hand, as vigilant guardians of the emerging
Plants from all predators — animal and human alike.
They now stand, hand in hand, as they reap
The bounty which nature has provided. The
Little garden now is a constant reminder
That their flee to freedom has provided the
Families with a future free from fear — protected
By a collective commitment to liberty.

A Clarion Call

From the mountains
They came.

From the prairies
They came.

From the sea shores
They came.

From the cities
They came.

From the farms
They came.

All to ring the bell.
To send a clarion call
For freedom and equality
For all.

To join in solidarity with
Earth's citizenry to stand
Tall against those who would
Destroy it all — In attempts to
Beat the weak and small unable
To defend themselves.

To be resolute in their efforts
To protect all who dare to seek
Freedom's call.

1963 — Trying to Fulfill an Assignment

It was a time of awakening in America.
A time which meant so much to me and
For our Generation.

A time which sprang from the innocence
Of the decade before — recovering from
The insanity of world wars.

One which had begun to focus inward
To the nurturing of those of the "baby boom"
Generation amidst evolving civil strife.

A time when the Nation began to pay
The price of systemic racial injustice
Created by generations of societal neglect
And no collective solutions — exasperated by
State sanctioned segregation.

It was in this historical time warp that
A boy sat alone in a small rural high school
Classroom late at night determined to join
The fight.

He needed to write a so-called "honors paper".
The assignment was clear. The students were to
Select a topic which would somehow connect the
Writings of American literature into a coherent analysis
Of no more than ten typewritten pages
For their demanding teacher.

The entire building was locked up tight.
Indeed, no one was permitted to be in
The school at such a late hour. But the boy
Had received permission from the school
Principal. He understood that, unlike most of the
Students in this class, the purchase of
A typewriter was beyond the boy's familial
Economic potential.

So, the principal made an exception to allow
Him to use the school's "typewriter room" —
As long as his decision remained private and
Between the two of them.

Thoughts of Mark Twain's *Tom Sawyer* and
The writings of Henry Wadsworth Longfellow's
Evangeline were the first works which came to
The boy's mind.

But he thought — it was time.
He could not retreat to the great writers
Of the past. At last, the injustices of today
must be discussed. So, he walked the
The dark hallways of the school to its small
Library in search of more contemporary authors.

He had seen these two books before. They were
Packed in with other volumes which
Seemed to have never been removed or
Explored.

The books he selected were placed on the
Shelf in a section entitled — "Miscellaneous".
He pulled the books and returned to the classroom
Filled with typewriters.

He was convinced that the books he had selected
Would provide the insights that would underscore
The central theme of his emerging paper.

As he picked away at the typewriter that night
He thought that the books he had chosen may
Not reflect the assignment's requirements. But
He was determined — he simply did not care.

After a week of long nights in the school and
Rewrite after rewrite, the boy presented his
"honors paper" to his teacher and class.

He read the experiences documented by
John Howard Griffin in, *Black Like Me*, and
The sadness and injustice of apartheid depicted
By Alan Paton in, *Cry My Beloved Country*.

The class sat silently and with some exasperation.
The presentation certainly did not fit the expected
Requirements of the assignment and was a sharp
Departure from those already delivered.

Indeed, discussions of race and discrimination rarely
Occurred in this homogeneous small Caucasian rural
Community. Therefore, the thought of delivering an
"honors paper" entitled — *Let My People Go* — was
Unexpected — to say the least.

It, therefore, was with some trepidation that the
Boy awaited the teacher's classroom evaluation.

To his relief and surprise, the instructor provided
Her analysis with tears in her eyes.

She explained to the class that she too felt
The pain that discrimination brings to each of
Us. And she apologized for being remiss at not
Offering the writings of wonderful contemporary
Authors which tell the stories of oppression. She
Promised that the next lesson would begin to address
That oversight.

Later, when asked why she was touched by the boy's
Paper, she responded, "I am the great granddaughter of
A man who fought for Abolition and the right for all men
To be free. It is my obligation to not stand aside, as I have
For too long, when injustice is right in front of me."

I am now reminded of what Martin believed —
"…that the arc of the moral universe is long, but it
Bends toward justice."

May this school lesson not be forgotten in the
twenty-third year of this century.

Accepting the Mission

What a struggle it is sometimes to navigate
The hate spread by those filled with
Grievance — trying to place the blame for
Their circumstances on the "others" — always
Failing to recognize that we are all sisters
And brothers encased in this temporary reality
Struggling to find our individual path for personal
Growth and security.

There exists a powerful temptation to respond
In kind. To cast them aside and find a place
To hide from their negativity.

Yet, for those who think and remember the words
Of the "seers" who have come before, we must
Fight the temptation of fleeing into our protected
Social worlds and to not confront the darkness that
Has been spun.

We must be brave enough not to submit to the
Evil that corrupted power creates and stand resolute
In a collective effort to defeat the darkness that
Ignorance breeds.

The Nightmare Continues

The building shakes. The baby cries.
The walls crumble — flames arise.
The terror of the night arrives.

The couple search for gramma
Amongst the rubble. Screams are
Heard throughout the building — sirens
Roar.

The missiles have brought the
Nightly death and destruction
Once more.

The "special operation" hits once again
Striking innocent women and children.
The nightmare continues.

Is anyone listening? Have we become
So hardened to the terror that we have
Forgotten that to subdue the evil in
The world that the Children of Light
Must stand up and fight?

How many must be sacrificed before
We decide that every child on this
Planet has an inalienable right to
Sleep without fear through the night?

Time to Stand and Be Counted

Trying to be the spark to ignite the torch.
Knowing that the time is coming to pass
The baton to others who also understand
The gravity of the circumstances surrounding
Our democracy.

Pleading for nuance and historical understanding
Of totalitarianism and its vicious killing fields
Strewn with unsuspecting souls bound by their own
Illiteracy and noncommittal to principles
Of tolerance — unwilling to be concerned with
The abuse of the "others". Leaving the heavy
Task of dissent to those few who accept the
Risks for the defense of liberty's call.

They watch from the shadows — praying that the darkness will
Not find them amongst their few remaining bobbles.

What can one say to them? That there will come
A day when they will pay the price for their continuing
Complicity in the destruction of Democracy.

A Plea

Speaking to an empty room.
Words seeking an audience.
Trying to challenge the darkness
That ignorance breeds.

Crying out to those willing to
Listen. Accepting the mission
So long ago given, "Forgive them
Father, for they know not what
They do."

Where to go from here? What messages
Can be sent? How to explain that they have
Become subservient to the manipulators of the
The truth — misled by the grifters and tyrants
Who prey on their fears and grievances.

Becoming hardened by the purveyors of
Half-truths and calculated misrepresentations
Sold for coins of the realm. Overwhelmed by
Propaganda and hate. Making the worst mistake.

Clinging to the words of those who distort the teachings
Of the masters who came before in an effort to claim
Righteousness — when the opposite is true.

False prophets all.
Oh, countrymen, countrymen, stand tall against
Those who would divide us all. Look to those who
Are truly sending a clarion call for us to join them
In their fight for freedom. And the right for the
Children to sleep without fear into the night.

Let us all reject the hatred and doom preached
By those who have corrupted the faith so long
Ago given.

Youth

Oh, the struggles of youth.
Constantly searching for the
Truth. Testing the integrity
Of others.

Experiencing Earth's
Wonders. Failing and then
Discovering the strength to
Recover. Fighting to stay open.
And learning how to recognize
Sincerity from gratuitous applause.

Finding other-regarding causes — all
In an effort to fulfill the Soul's call
This time around the Sun.

What a wondrous time to begin
The journey and experience the beauty
Which Mother Nature provides. Regardless
Of the inevitable mistakes which may occur,
Let us all celebrate the majesty and energy of
Youth.

Searching for Balance

Searching for Balance

Between unwritten lines. Yearning for
Better times. Encased by obligation.
Completing the mission — the lonely
Soul seeks to be fulfilled and to be
Given permission to find redemption.

Images of days past compete for recognition
And applause. They resurrect sweet
Remembrances of youth. Of days wrapped in
The arms of the one who sacrificed all to
To bring the searching soul across the void
Into form and to experience the warmth of
Everlasting love.

Torn between the ought and the is.
Trying to make sense of it all. Shocked by
The hate and vitriol that ignorance breeds.
Searching for a sanctuary but finding none.

Yet, recognizing that the time has come to
Confront the darkness with the power of
Unyielding love — in the quest for equilibrium.

Transitions

Born into loving illiteracy.
Insulated from familial tragedies.
Struggling to overcome a predetermined
Destiny.

Surrounded by bias and jealousy
A great equalizer was found which
Transformed economic insecurity
And social class through objective
Performance into success.

Physical and individual sacrifice
Provided a pathway to escape
The bigotry and hate which surrounded
Him and many others — trapped in the cycles
Of generational tragedies.

Each phase of the journey required some
Form of re-invention. From athlete to academic
To loneliness created in an effort to help the
Evolution of the one loved so deeply.

It was understood that each personal transition
Required a commitment to a new mission
Dependent upon a recognition that each stage
In the soul's evolution was necessary to fulfill
Obligations long ago created.

Trying now to complete the circle.
Reaching out to lost
Friends and love ones in an effort
To find peace this time around the
Sun.
Confident that he will be welcomed
By others whose new transitions have
Already begun.

A Nightly Visitor

She came in the night from
Memories wrapped tight
Packed in emotions flowing
From the soul's evolution.

She was surrounded by beautiful
Sounds — Like notes of a Chopin
Piano concerto awakening every
Part of my being. Reminding me that
My time may be fleeting — but that I
Have been granted more opportunities
To wander amongst Mother Earth's beauty.

If only I remain open and understand
That the paths before me are eternal —
Filled with love everlasting.

Escaping Self

Dig deep and you will find
A place where you can escape
All the fears that have found
Their way into your heart — which
Are slowly tearing your dreams apart.

Start with the quiet sound of one
Hand clapping — until you hear nothing
But your soul sending messages to you
That all is well if you simply trust the
Agreement once constructed.

Remember the covenant created by
Those who came before which described
The path which must be followed to insure
That your world will be filled with love and
How to overcome hate.

Listen — Open the door — It is a gift
Given to you — for ever more.

A Chance Meeting

I met a man the other day
Who inadvertently crossed my
Way.

He stopped suddenly when he
Realized that we almost collided.
He humbly asked for my forgiveness —
But I quickly responded that the fault
Was equally mine.

At that moment we both recognized
That the day would be much brighter
Now that we realized the importance
of life without recrimination.

And, the satisfaction that kindness brings
To all things — and the need for redemption.

The Quiet of the Night

The beautiful stillness of the night
Can quiet the restless spirit and
Help remind us of the paths by which
We can open the door.

It reminds us not to lose sight of
Our roles in the eternal cycles of life.

It can connect us, if we wish, to the
Messages of those who have come
Before.

The silence pulsates through moonbeams
And sparkling shooting stars — showering
Our dreams with cosmic energy. It leads us
Through earthly trials and tribulations with
Celestial rhythms of everlasting love.

May we all welcome the quiet of the night.

A Lesson learned

"It has been all written before," said the student
To his Mentor.
"Yes, but not by you Son," replied the Mentor. "There
Remains much to be done. Not for the ribbons, but
For the children. They are empty vessels in need to
To be filled with love and empathy. It is your task
To help them see.

Hate is learned not inherited.
Yet, it continues to burn within the hearts of too
Many. Love must overcome if the mission assigned
To us is to be ultimately won."

The student asked, "What becomes of those who
Reject this wisdom?"

The Mentor responded, "Sadly, they will be overcome
By the darkness they spread. Trapped by their evil web.
Caught in their never-ending vitriol and venom — left with
Everlasting rejection and depression."

Even though decades have passed — this lesson
Must not be forgotten. May we all stop and listen.

Remain Engaged

It comes like a silent agitator
Picking and prodding — reminding
Us not to lose sight of the challenges
Ahead.

To continue to document that which
Has been left unsaid. Always pushing
Us to remain open and willing to
Answer the call.

To be hell bent and unrelenting
In the fight to maintain our individual
And collective freedom.

To continue to aspire to achieve
The rewards which have been
Secured long ago. To do so with
Love and compassion. Yet strong
Enough to be unwilling to submit
To the forces of darkness and greed.

Like the emerging sunlight after
A fierce storm, our inner-self reminds
Us of the power we have to overcome
All obstacles — if we remain open — willing
To understand that we must answer Mother
Nature's call to protect all creatures
Great and small as we travel through
On our journeys in this time and space.

No Rest Tonight

The vessel is dry.
Every last thought
Has been sought and
Memorialized. Every
Message has been sent
To those willing to listen.

The obligation that once was secured
Has been fulfilled. At least
That is what the man thought.

But, alas, the door which was
Slowly closing, suddenly has been
Blown open once again. Reminding
Him that the mission had not been
Accomplished.

No matter how much he tried to
Forget, millions of Earth's citizens
Live in fear — starvation remains near for them.
The planet teeters on the precipice of
Catastrophic climate destruction
Demanding governmental co-operation.

The vessel must be filled again
As long as the words can be found
To encourage the Children of Light
To continue the fight for what they
Understand to be necessary and right.

There will be no sleep tonight until
The Vessel slowly fills to the brim again with
Renewed messages to send.

Evolving

Surrounded in uncertainty
Engulfed by the currents of obligation
Struggling not to drown — grasping for
Answers — dreaming they will be found
Hidden amongst the currents of memories
Deeply embedded in the Soul's evolution.

Fighting against the fear of the unknown.
Yet, determined to sail into the wind with
The wisdom obtained from years of epiphanies
Discovered. Committed to share with other
Seekers also crying for love — trying to find
Their way.

Each choice provides unintended undertones
Which may sweep away the joy that resurrected
Love can bring.

Trying to find the silver chalice which will
Bring eternal happiness to lost souls.
Seeking oneness and a loving finality
To the games.

Flying

Sailing the cosmos
Like a ship on the crest
Of a wave.

Trying to catch a message
Along the Milky Way.

Tapping into the pulsating
Rhythms long ago created.

Looking for answers hidden
Within the mysterious backdrop
Of the celestial play.

Finding glimpses of wisdom
Scattered within. Confident
That many more will be given.

The City of Gold

On the road to eternity
The man struggled to see
That the golden city at the
End of his travels was much
Closer than he believed.

But he began to understand that the
Towering buildings of gold he had imagined
Were mere illusions created
By his own confusion
Of what was meant to be.

He slowly came to the conclusion
That the treasures he was seeking
Already surrounded him.
He began to appreciate the beauty
Of the meadows standing before
Him — filled with brilliant
Yellow sunflowers standing proudly
With their faces turned to the afternoon
Light.

He now noticed the crystal blue water
Gently flowing in the little stream
In between the earthen embankments created
By its steady travels to the sea.

Could it be, he thought, that in his haste
To find the city of gold that he
Had failed to recognize the treasures
Which had been laid before him
By Mother Nature's majesty?

As he pondered the folly of his
Journey, he heard a voice softly
Whispering — "You have already
Arrived. This is your sanctuary.
Protect it. Help others see the
Indescribable beauty that you
Have discovered. Help them in
Their struggles to be free."

No longer does the man search
For the artificial bobbles produced
By those blinded by their own greed.

Instead, without recrimination, he
Encourages, nudges, and pleads for
Them to join him and others who
Are determined to protect Nature's
Sanctuary.

Shadows of the Night

A candle that once glowed bright
Lighting the darkness from the night
Now flickers in the room seeking more
And more attention. It pushes back from
Its inevitable fate. Trying to fight
The darkness until morning's light.

The flames cast shadows on the walls
Creating images of beautiful ballerinas
Dancing across the room — knowing that
The symphony will end soon. But willing
To perform until Dawn brings the curtain
Down.

They are confident in the messages they
Have sent — their only hope is that they will be found.

The Space Within

In between dreams
And promises kept.
Love finds a way to
Guide us through
To secure the steps
Which must be performed
To find peace amongst
The warm glow of souls
Seeking to become one.

Appreciation

What is it that makes a man
Thrust aside all Nature's treasures
For some ephemeral pleasure?

Is it hedonistic pride? Is it some hidden
Desire to self-destruct or to unthinkingly
Believe that he can reconstruct that which
Has been given to him in an attempt to
Control the universe?

Those who work the land understand
The need to nurture the soil. To pamper
It with Nature's nutrients. And to recognize
That regardless of their sweat and toil, that
No amount of manufactured chemicals can
Replace the dependence that each cultivated
Field has upon Mother Nature's co-operation.

How hard is it to understand and show some
Appreciation?

Words

Words flowing from the vessel
Shaped by loving hands eons ago
Presented to show the majesty
Of our lives — as we journey through
Our time.

They act as pathfinders offering
Glimpses of what road to take
As we make our way through
Each day — reminding us that we
Are but passengers on this ride through
The Milky Way.

We place word after word in some decipherable
Order in an effort to catch the attention of others
Who are also along for the ride.

Each word sends a message from our souls.
Like shooting stars in the night sky, words can be
Beams of light filled with love and compassion.
They are brief reminders that there is much
More to come.

They challenge us to dig deep beyond the
Superficial — to discover the paths that we
Must take to join in the celebration of life —
Offered to us this time in space.

One Life's Journey

Seeing without looking.
Hearing without listening.
Flying without destination.

Loving without reservation.
Finding universal oneness
Without fear.

Searching for balance.
Leaving, learning
Rejecting the mirror.

Recovering from the
Vitriol and hate.
Trying to help others
Not to make the mistake.

Receiving ribbons and prizes
But becoming wiser as to what
Is truly important in the game.

On Being Quiet

There is a time in each day
When we can no longer play
The assigned role which circumstance
Has required us to perform.

When whatever job description we have
Attached to our names must be set
Aside. And once again become quiet —
And listen.

When we must search for the wonderful
Rhythms pulsating within and without us.

A time when we must open the door
And allow our inner self to soar.

To reach beyond the images in the
Mirror and join in celebration with
The universal givens implanted throughout
The celestial seasons.

It is then that we will find our Soul's
Demands — offering us gentle commands
As to our individual prerequisites for
Lasting peace and happiness.

Completing the Circle

Where are the dreams of yesterday?
Where have they gone?

Are they hidden amongst the horrors
Of wars fought long ago? Or, the betrayals
Of lost loves so thoughtlessly performed?

Where is the love so beautifully conceived
Shaped in the caverns of my memories now
Screaming to be retrieved?

They lie down in the golden meadows
Amongst the fallen leaves — sowed by
Love's longing one day too long ago — still
Planted deep within my soul.

There are regrets — trying not
To forget. Driven by the knowledge
That experience begets.

Finding ways to set the sorrows aside
In an effort to overcome the obstacles
Thrust from without and within.

Trying to pay homage to all who
Have come before and for those
Who come after.
Reminded by the powerful words
That "We shall overcome."

Understanding that too many have
Sacrificed their lives for justice not
To be done.

The Stream

There once was a man
Of advanced maturity who
Constantly sought clarity
In a world filled with confusion
And contradiction.

He sought answers to unanswerable
Questions. Always searching for
Suggestions from those confident
In their analyses.

But, time after time, he walked away
Dissatisfied and disillusioned.

One day he came upon a child sitting
Beside a little stream. He was fishing
With just a stick and string.

The man was intrigued by the boy's
Angelic demeanor. So, he stopped
And thought, "I wonder what insight
A child could provide in my endless
Quest for answers?"

At his wits' end he decided, to at least,
Be polite and exchange pleasantries
Then continue his walk. But what he
Thought would be a brief encounter
Lasted much longer.

The little boy was no more than seven,
Or maybe eight — a child who had not
Confronted a world filled with hate.

He possessed a cherub like face
With eyes that matched the most
Beautiful blue sky ever created.
He radiated a sense of calmness and
Empathy rarely experienced by the Man.

So, the Man began to ask a few questions.
"Do you expect to catch fish with only a
Stick and string for a line and a hook made
From a paperclip?"

The child responded, "Well, its all I have. But
It will be enough. The stream and I are friends.
It has told me to be patient and to sit and wait.
And that the worm I have used as bait will provide
Me with dinner tonight."

The man smiled and asked, "Do you speak often to
The stream?"

"Oh, yes, almost every day. It has taught me
Many things. It will speak to you, too. But you
Must remain still," the boy replied.

"Listen to it gently circling around the big
Rock over there. Do you see it forming
A pool by the embankment? It has created
A sanctuary for the fish needing to escape
Its current." The boy continued.

Bewildered by the boy's observations the
Man asked, "Why do fish need a resting spot?
Don't they enjoy the excitement of the current
As it rushes toward its final destination with the
Sea?"

"Well, the stream has told me that fish, like men,
Need to also stop and recognize their part in the
Endless process that they are privileged to play.
And to be vigilant not to be swept away by the
Power of the current — as they make their way
In fulfilling their predestined obligation to find
Safety as they give birth and complete their roles
In Mother Nature's play." The boy responded.

In awe of the child's responses, the Man asked
One last question. "How do you know such
Things?"

The boy smiled and responded, "The stream
Told me. You, too, will find your answers if
You sit beside me and — listen."

About the Author

Steven O. Ludd, Lawyer/Professor Emeritus, is the author of numerous legal and professional publications. Additionally, he has written a well-received book of poetry, *Reflections Off the Lake, Poems on Life, Love, and Democracy.*

In *Walking the Property Line: Messages From Nature's Sanctuary*, he returns to a theme central in all his poetic observations — the protection of nature and its importance in the struggle for love to overcome hate.

After receiving his law degree and Ph.D. from Syracuse University's College of Law and the Maxwell School of Citizenship and Public Affairs, he began a thirty year teaching career at Bowling Green State University. Additionally, he served the United States Federal Court as both a Federal Court Monitor and as an Alternative Dispute Mediator and Arbitrator.

www.ingramcontent.com/pod-product-compliance
Lightning Source LLC
LaVergne TN
LVHW051154080426
835508LV00021B/2620